Feelings

Jealous

Sarah Medina

Illustrated by Jo Brooker

Raintree

www.raintreepublishers.co.uk
Visit our website to find out more information about **Raintree** books.

To order:
 Phone 44 (0) 1865 888112
 Send a fax to 44 (0) 1865 314091
Visit the Raintree Bookshop at **www.raintreepublishers.co.uk** to browse our catalogue and order online.

First published in Great Britain by Raintree,
Halley Court, Jordan Hill, Oxford OX2 8EJ,
part of Harcourt Education.
Raintree is a registered trademark of
Harcourt Education Ltd.

Editorial: Daniel Nunn, Cassie Mayer and
  Diyan Leake
Design: Joanna Hinton-Malivoire and
  Ron Kamen
Illustrations: Jo Brooker
Picture research: Erica Newbery
Production: Duncan Gilbert

Originated by Modern Age
Printed and bound in China by
  South China Printing Company

ISBN: 978 1 4062 0637 1 (hardback)
11 10 09 08 07
10 9 8 7 6 5 4 3 2 1

ISBN: 978 1 4062 0644 9 (paperback)
12 11 10 09 08
10 9 8 7 6 5 4 3 2 1

British Library Cataloguing in Publication Data
Medina, Sarah
Feelings: Jealous
152.4'8

A full catalogue record for this book is available
from the British Library.

Acknowledgements
The publishers would like to thank the following
for permission to reproduce photographs:
Bananastock p. **22C, D**; Corbis p. **12** (bottom),
p**14, 18**; Getty Images/photodisc p. **12** (top);
Getty Images/Taxi p. **22B**; Punchstock/Photodisc
p. **22A**.

Every effort has been made to contact copyright
holders of any material reproduced in this book.
Any omissions will be rectified in subsequent
printings if notice is given to the publishers.

Contents

Some words are shown in bold, **like this**. They are explained in the glossary on page 23.

What is jealousy?

Jealousy is a **feeling**. Feelings are something you feel inside. Everyone has different feelings all the time.

happy

angry

sad

If you are jealous, you may think that other people have got more than you. You might want what they have got.

What happens when I am jealous?

When you are jealous, you might feel sad and **lonely**. You may not want to talk or play.

6

Being jealous can also make you feel angry. You might feel like saying or doing unkind things.

Why do people feel jealous?

People feel jealous for all kinds of reasons. They may want something that someone else has got.

Some children feel jealous of their brother or sister. They may think that a baby gets all the **attention**.

Is it OK to feel jealous?

Jealousy is a normal feeling. Everyone feels jealous sometimes.

It is not good to stay jealous for too long. It is much better to be happy for other people.

What can I do when I am jealous?

If you feel jealous, tell someone. Talk to a parent or teacher. They will understand.

Remember everything that you do well.
You might not be the best at painting,
but you could be a great model-maker!

Will I always feel jealous?

All **feelings** change over time. You
will not feel jealous for ever.

Try being kind to the person you are jealous of. Soon you will both feel happy!

How can I tell if someone is jealous?

People who feel jealous may seem angry. They may hurt you by saying or doing mean things.

Jealousy can make people feel sad
or **lonely**. They may not want to play
with anyone.

17

Can I help when someone is jealous?

You can help someone who is jealous. Be kind to them. Invite them to play with you.

Tell them that you like them. Then they will know that you want to be their friend.

I feel better now!

Remember, everyone feels jealous sometimes. If you know what to do with jealous **feelings**, they will soon pass.

Everyone is special in different ways, and that includes you! Be happy with yourself, just as you are.

What are these feelings?

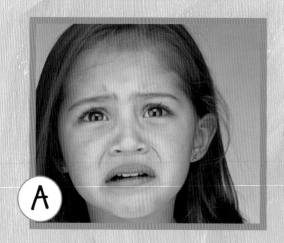

A

B

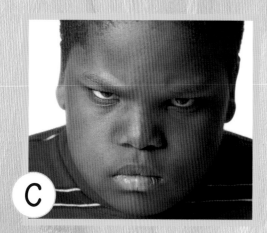

C

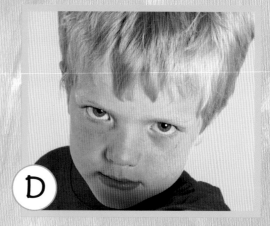

D

Which of these people look happy?
What are the other people feeling?
Look at page 24 to see the answers.

Picture glossary

attention

when someone spends time talking to another person or doing things with them

feeling

something that you feel inside. Jealousy is a feeling.

lonely

when you feel all alone. Loneliness is a feeling.

Index

Answers to questions on page 22

The person in picture B looks happy. The other people could be sad, angry, or lonely.

Note to Parents and Teachers

Reading for information is an important part of a child's literacy development. Learning begins with a question about something. Help children think of themselves as investigators and researchers by encouraging their questions about the world around them. Most chapters in this book begin with a question. Read the question together. Look at the pictures. Talk about what you think the answer might be. Then read the text to find out if your predictions were correct. Think of other questions you could ask about the topic, and discuss where you might find the answers. Assist children in using the picture glossary and the index to practice new vocabulary and research skills.